Written By
Isreba Wheeler
aka
Hope Syndreamz

Illustrated By
Sky Owens
aka
Art Werx

"Amir's First Haircut"

The Ongoing Saga Of Life's Lessons Through the Eyes of a Young Boy

#4

Amir's First Haircut

Published by Dumplinz Book Publishing

BRONX, NY 10467

(917) 642-5549 isreba1949@gmail.com

hopesyndreamz@gmail.com

www.dumplinzbookpublishing.com

Isreba Wheeler Aiken, Publisher/Editorial Director

Yvonne Rose/Quality Press.info, Book Packager

Sky Owens, Cover and Interior Illustrator

ALL RIGHTS RESERVED

No part of this book may be reproduced or transmitted in any form or by any means–electronic or mechanical, including photocopying, recording or by any information storage and retrieval system without written permission from the authors, except for the inclusion of brief quotations in a review. Requests for permission or further information should be addressed to "The Permissions Department," hopesyndreamz@gmail.com or isreba1949@gmail.com

Dumplinz Books are available at special discounts for bulk purchases, sales promotions, fund raising or educational purposes. For details, contact: Special Sales Department, Dumplinz Book Publishing, (917) 642-5549 / hopesyndreamz@gmail.com or isreba1949@gmail.com

Text Copyright © 2019 by Dumplinz Book Publishing

Illustrations Copyright © 2019 by Sky Owens

Paperback ISBN #: 978-0- 9964684-7-3

Hardcover ISBN #: 978-0- 9964684-9-7

Ebook ISBN #: 978-0- 9964684-8-0

Library of Congress Control Number: 2018965310

Dedication

Dedication to the memory of our sweetest cousin... *Geneva Pritchett*.

She was the kind of young lady that brightened a room once entered.

She has not left my memory, and it is for that reason...

I dedicate this book to my beautiful Cousin...*Geneva*.

To everyone presently suffering from Lupus...

Don't...Stop...Fighting.

We believe in you.

Here's a little story I want to share with you all.
It's about my first haircut; and why my head is bald.

But Daddie had a talk with me. He said 'men should be neat. A man's hair should not be so long; it reaches to his feet.'

Sooo, after a few days of pouting, I gave up; Daddie was right. I'm going to have my hair cut in two weeks, on a Saturday night.

I went to school and told my friends, but their faces grew sad. Most of them cut their hair already; they said ...it was bad.

Natalie told us that she went
to a very nice hair salon.
Her mom had her hair trimmed
down short, 'cause it was really long.

She said she cried and cried all day,
she didn't want them to do it.
But her mom said it takes too long
to detangle then shampoo it.

Next day at school the kids were cruel;
called her mean names of sorts.
They kept calling Natalie a boy
because her hair was so short.

But once we found out that she was
being called all of those names -
we stopped them quick, cause name
calling is bullying; it's all the same.

Kennii said he ran and hid, 'they were not going to get me.' But since his hair is very short, they got their way, I see.

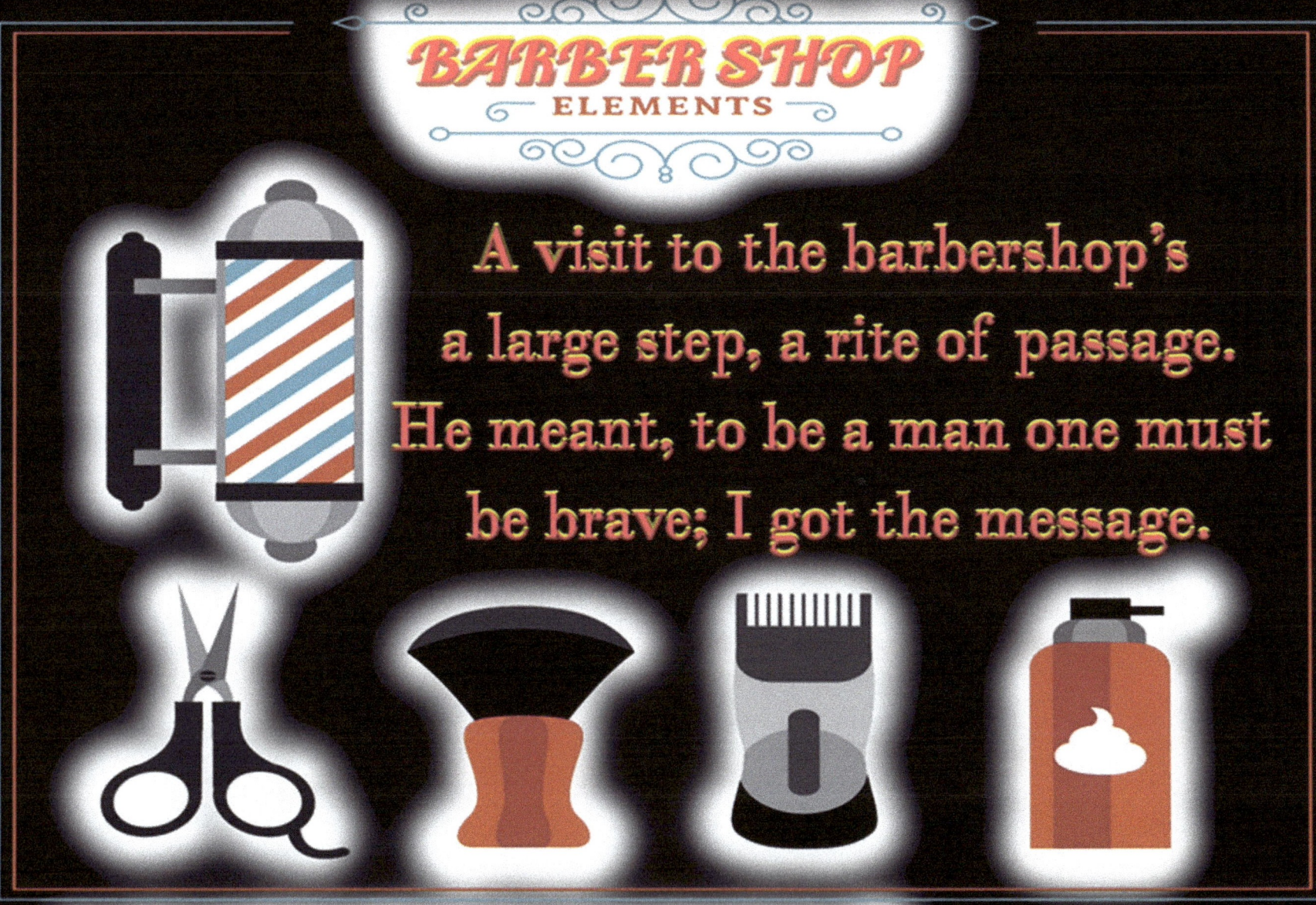

I calmed my nerves
and then I learned
another friend of mine...
...who sits beside me
every day's been
absent for a long time.

Her name is Geneva
and when you meet her,
you would like her a lot.
She's friendly, fun,
laughs a bunch, one of
the bestest friends I've got.

We used to eat lunch every day, we'd share our treats and stuff.

I'd always trade my sweet treats for her mom's homemade cream puffs.

Still,
we remained
the best of friends...
even though sight unseen.
She
still considered
me her pal,
our friendship's peachy keen.

But after time I began to notice she was always coming in late. She always looked so pale and sick, like maybe her tummy ached.

And then I didn't see her come to class for a long long time. And she missed a whole bunch of tests; I hope she's feeling fine.

I called her on the phone one day; she missed another test. Her Aunt Patti said she was ill, and needed some more rest.

Our friends kept asking; 'Where's Geneva? She hasn't been in school.' I told them she was really sick, and that she'll return soon.

Then, I said, "HEY! WAIT! A GET-WELL card, will make her face shine!!

We'll tell her close friends, and the whole class, so they too can sign!!"

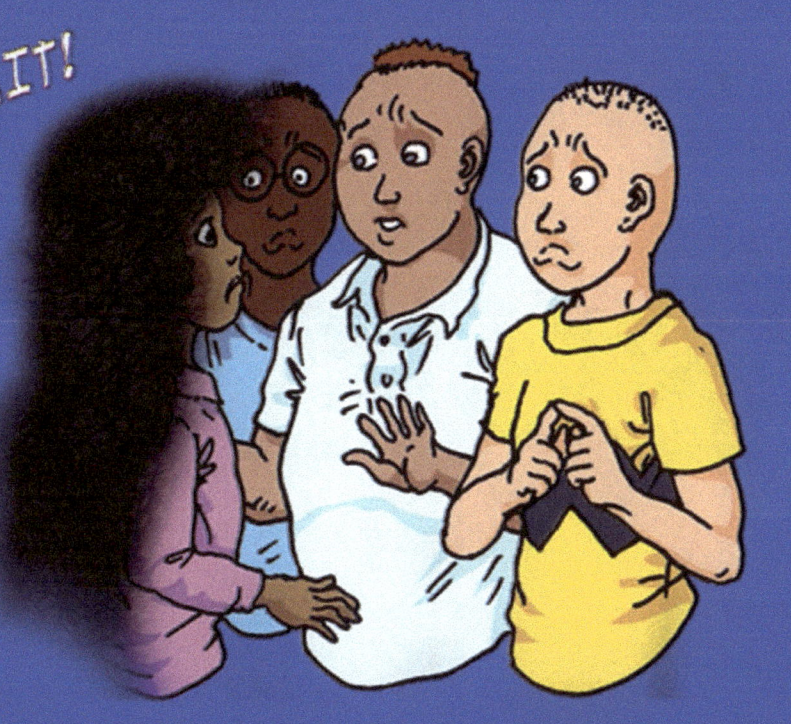

So we all got together and
made her a great big card.
We drew, colored, and made
it pretty...it wasn't too hard.

We showed it to our teacher,
and she passed it all around.
So many people signed it,
not an empty space to be found.

And when school was finished for the day,

I ran outside.

I ran right to Geneva's house to show our card with pride!

I took it to her house for her to see how much we care.
But when I rang, I heard a soft voice say no one was there.
I stood there for a moment; I did not know what else to do.
I told the voice, "It's a card for Geneva; you'll give it to her, won't you?"
I saw the curtain on the locked door sway in the wind a little.
The door unlocked a hand appeared with nails very short and brittle.

"Yes, I will make sure she receives this. Thank you and goodbye."

Yanno...that voice sounds real familiar, but I don't know why!

But that soft voice was so familiar,
my mind played it again.
Then without a doubt,
I began to shout,
"HEY... THAT WAS MY FRIEND!"

I ran back to Geneva's house, and knocked and knocked and knocked. A soft voice said, "Ok...I'm coming," and then the door unlocked.

I stood there staring face to face, at my very sick little friend. She looked so pale, hair under a veil then she said, "Come on in."

Inside... the house was very dim, and all of the curtains were drawn. Sunrays would sneak between creases to shine in, but not for very long. I walked behind her, and stepped inside her room like many times before. She walked straight ahead, climbed into her bed, and quietly I closed her door.

"How have you been Geneva? We have not seen you at school. I hope you liked the card we made, everyone signed it too."

She smiled at me while nodding her head; almost as if she was well. She coughed a little, cleared her throat, and said,
"Thank you....it was swell."

"I'm glad you liked it Geneva, the kids miss you in the yard. They think about your funny jokes, and we'd laugh long and hard."

She giggled softly, batted her lashes and said, "Where is your lunch? I really miss trading my cream puff snacks, I really miss it a bunch."

I said,

"I'll gladly go and get you some, if that is what you'd like."

She smiled then rubbed her tummy a lot, "I couldn't eat a bite."

I said to her,

"Are you sick from something you ate before?"

She shook her head, and said instead, "No, it's much much more."

"Everything was fine 'til one day at school, I felt very sick. The school nurse called my Ma'am–Mother, and said...

"Try to come quick!

I think it would be wise for you to take her to the hospital today."

Ma'am–Mother came, spoke to the nurse, then we were on our way."

"We left the school right then and there to see my primary physician. Afterwards, ma'am—mother and Aunt Patti spoke softly in the kitchen.

I went to bed and after a while they both came in to see me. They told me I was very sick, and that they'd never leave me.

We'd stick it out together, and they'd be there through and through. I told them that I loved them. They said, "That's what families do."

I smiled at her and she smiled back,
as we sat there in silence.
I don't know why, I didn't cry,
I just wanted to be quiet.

My friend Geneva's very sick,
that made me feel real sad.
I sat as she explained to me,
just what it was she had.

"You see... I have Systemic Lupus, and I've had it for a while.
It can affect you as an adult, or you can get it as a child.
Five to Ten thousand kids get Lupus every year.
And, I am one of them, Amir; that's why I'm resting here.
Affects Asian and Black people more so than any other races.
And sometimes you go through hair loss; that is... in some cases.
There is no cure for Systemic Lupus, the goal is to control.
So I hope to be by your side my friend as together, we grow old.

Sometimes I get chest pains whenever I would take a deep breath.
So, when I'm not at school, I'm really tired, I need more rest.
I sometimes have bad pains in my heart; at times it skips a beat.
My tummy hurts quite often; and feels nauseous after I eat.
The sunlight always hurts my eyes, and so I am forced to wear a cap.
My hair has thinned; falling out, not growing in; so... I keep it wrapped."

"Is that why you're sitting here with me, wearing that big red scarf?"

"Yes... I have huge bald patches in the front and in other parts."

"So why don't you just come to school, like that, maybe wearing a shawl?"

"I wanted to go, but it scared me so, I couldn't go to school at all."

But, what is Lupus? I thought to myself.
I didn't have a clue.
I had to find out right away, I needed
my parents to talk to.

Then I thought maybe Geneva didn't
know just how to tell me.
So when I got home I asked Mommie
if we could have a "talky."

We call it that when we need to get
something off our chest.
We have a talky, go for a walky and
then put it to rest.

But Mom said, "Wait for dad's return,
he'll be home tonight.
And we'll be sure to talk it out
before we say goodnight."

Daddie came home just in time, I was feeling a bit worried.
He saw my face, picked up his pace; he knew he had to hurry.

Mommie sat me on her lap, and spoke to me soft and sweetly, "Sweetheart, Geneva is quite sick." Mommie said she would need me. I looked into my Daddie's eyes and whispered, "She'll be okay? I went to see her, Daddie, but she looked very sad today."

"Not quite so sad as she's feeling bad, her body's quite confused.

Her fighting cells aren't doing well; they're fighting whom they choose."

I smiled at Mommie and she knew I really didn't understand. Then Daddie placed me on his lap, and he held up his hand.

"Imagine son"...dad said seriously..."I gave you balloons to pop. You're only allowed to pop the ones with the red X painted on top. But if I covered up your eyes with a blindfold, you can't tell. You'd pop every balloon you'd touch, thinking you did your job well."

"Inside us all we have a large posse; they're called the immune system. And when our body's invaded with germs they fight to rid us of them. They send out antibody soldiers to fight against those bad bacteria. And when they're done, we can have fun; they've restored the sick area."

"But in Geneva's body, even a cold is very bad.
So, she must stay at home a lot so her system won't feel sad.

I guess their eyes are covered too,
so they can't see what they're doin.'
And when the war ends, Geneva
feels pain from the good areas that
they've ruined.

And that is why Geneva is sick;
her good cells are under attack.
They're blindly fighting the cells inside
her, and those cells can't fight back.

So now you can understand Geneva's
plight, her system's a little off whack.
Her antibodies aren't doing their job;
it's her good cells they constantly attack."

"Even though this is a disease,
we won't ever push her away from us.
Not all diseases are catchy, my love,
and this one is not contagious.

So when you see your friend again,
walk up to her and give her a hug.
It's not easy being sick all the time;
it's good to know we're still loved.

Now a lot might change for Geneva;
not going to school for instance.
But that's no reason to limit your friendship,
or to keep your distance.

You treat her as you always have,
your friend, your pal, your buddy.
When you need to, and if she's well enough;
go over to her house to study."

The two of them they kissed my head,

and hugged me: squeezed me firm.

I prayed that night she'd be alright;

to school she would return.

That next day was a Friday, and I talked to all our friends.
I told them of Geneva's plight: it saddened them to no end.

I told them I was going to get my haircut the next day.
I wanted it to be for her, they can shave it all away.

I'll shave my head to show support; I'll stand right by her side.
I'll come to school the next day and I'll wear my head with pride.

Our friends told me that's a great idea; her head she won't feel shame.
She has a friend who understands; 'cause my head will be the same.

I didn't tell my parents;
I made this decision on my own.
I want to support my dear friend,
so she won't feel alone.

It's Saturday morn, I'm at the shop with Daddie sitting cool.

But when I look up here comes
all of our friends from our school.

First came in I'Nauree,

and right behind
him came his dad.

He hopped up in
a chair near mine,

and smiled at me real glad.

Next entered Chris, Ryan, and Ayden;
they came rushing in.
They ran right up to us while yelling,
"We go after them!"

Chanse came in and lil Ken Murph
followed closely on his tail.
"We've come to help, she's our friend too,"
This plan will never fail.

And then the door swung open wide,
and Natalie walked in.

We were surprised to see her here;
this place she's never been.

We greeted her as she walked over to us saying,
"I want to help too."
It's already short but shaving it for
Geneva's the right thing to do."

We laughed and laughed my friends and me;
my fear was almost gone.
I had a lot of thick black hair,
but soon it would be gone.

My Daddie sat there wondering
why all of my friends had shown.
"We've decided to shave off all our hair
Daddie, so Geneva's not alone."

My Daddie smiled; tears in his eyes,
"Now you're sitting tall."
"Hey Barber Nash, I've got the cash,
I'm paying for them all."

Mr. Nash smiled called over six guys; then shaved us altogether.

My fear was gone, I felt real strong; my friends made me feel better.

Four Sundays and Mondays have passed
for school we could not wait.
We hoped she'd show so that she'd know
she's loved by her classmates.
The day flew by, and after lunch,
we came back to our classroom.
This day will end in a few hours;
I really hope she comes soon.

I smiled real bright
when from the dark
rose my friend in a head wrap.
With smiles real wide,
we rose from our seats,
and we began to clap.

She stopped and stared
'cause we had no hair,
it was a lovely sight.
With tears she relaxed,
thoughts of having no wrap
'cause now it felt alright.

Went to her desk
pulled out her chair,
and there Geneva stood.

But this time she
did not look sad; in fact,
she looked real good.

She turned and faced us...
each of us, and said,
"Why...why did you do it?"

I rose from my seat,
snapped my fingers saying,
"It's just hair...nothing to it."

"You are our friend Geneva, and we care about you a whole lot.
You will not go through this alone, you're the only you we've got.

It's only hair, and now that it's gone, you will not stand out."
She started to cry, as he asked why; "Now what are those tears all about?"

She said, "Thank you, now I'm not ashamed; I can come back to school once more.
Because of you all, I knew I belonged the minute I walked through the door.

No school, no fun, always feeling ill, I've had a lot on my plate.
I have been very sick for a while, but this made me feel great."

We made our friend feel good today,
a joy she almost lost.
All she needed was support from friends;
not too high a cost.

To battle something such as Lupus'
hard even for a child.
Although others are there for you,
the pain is there all the while.

Lupus is a stranger to people and known by very few.
In fact, some never heard the name…I was like that too.

Two-thirds of the world knows nothing about this disease.
So it creeps up on lots of folks, and brings them to their knees.

It's not discreet, real hard to treat, and no, there is no cure.
So if you know someone who has it, hold them tight for sure.

Cause it attacks all over the body, and anywhere that it pleases.
It won't just simply run its course like colds or some diseases.

You're at a greater risk if you're Black, Asian, Latin, or Native American.
And although it can affect both genders, it occurs in women more than men.

Okay…now you know my little tale of why my hair is bald.
I loved my hair, but she's my friend; no favor's too short or tall.

A true friend never hesitates; he's there even when he's not asked.
They do all they can, no matter the price; it's never too much of a task.

For friendship requires more than just fun,
sometimes you friend is in need.
And when they call, stand by their side
supporting with both…words and deeds.

But if your friend is sick;
they'll need you first to understand.
They may not call, but if they should fall,
be there to lend a hand.

When you have friends….true friends who need you,
always give support.
Your loving kindness shields them from all
harm just like a fort.

To give support means stand beside them, no matter the time or place.
It means you'll always be there lending your help no matter the case.

We love our friend Geneva,
and although her disease is her own.
We happily loan her our support
so she would not go it alone.

I hope you learned a little bit about Lupus and being supportive.
When you have friends who need your help, there's nothing you should not give.

If you have a friend who needs your support, then give it right away. You'll never know just how fantastic, you could make their day.

This story is written in the embraced memory of our litle cousin, "Geneva Pritchett," who surrendered under the powers of Lupus when she was a mere 21 yrs old. Her heart was as vast as the "Tarkine Forest of Tasmania." Life has not been the same without her, and the world revolves a little bit slower...but only for her family who truly knew and loved her, and for those friends who grew to truly know and love her.

Alberta Pritchett

Aka

Ma'am Mother

Patricia Pritchett-Alexander
"PATTY"

ISREBA WHEELER

SKY OWENS

CARPHETIS AIKEN

LEAH CROSS

Acknowledgements

Thank you, *Jehovah*, for providing me the ability to dive deep into my imagination and write what I see. Thank you, *Mommie-Juanita Wheeler*, for being the hand that guided me, encouraging me to never stop imagining. Thank you freepik.com for your original illustrations used as backgrounds for my pages in this book. Thank you to *Sketchepedia - Freepik.com* for a few of my background patterns. Thanks for the background images Created by *Kjpargeter - Freepik.com*. Thank you for the background images Created by *Starline - Freepik.com*. Thank you for the background images Created by *Harryarts - Freepik.com*. Thank you for the background images Created by *Starline - Freepik.com*. Thank you for the images Created by *Creative_hat - Freepik.com*. Although other background images I found were free on the internet, I still believe giving credit where it is due is beneficial for both parties involved, permitting others to learn where they too can go for such awesome background images.

Again...Thank you.

Thank you for sticking by me throughout this process, *Yvonne, and Tony Rose*. Without your gentle pushes, and constant reminders, this book would be forever in my mind, and eternally out of reach for children the world over. Nevertheless, due to your persistence, and belief in me, it has been brought to life, and all can learn from it, and its many morals. You will forever be, my Auntie & Uncle. I love you both.

Thank you once again, as I have done in every Dumplinz book, *John Blasingame* - Owner of *New Day Associates, Inc.*, for granting me the opportunity to hitch my cart to *Amber Communications Group, Inc*...and *Quality Press* owned by *Mr. & Mrs. Rose*. Without your kindness for such a priceless meet and greet of my new Auntie and Uncle...none of my Dumplinz Books would have been brought to life. I am forever grateful to you. I love you *Uncle B.* Thank you, *Shauna-BooDeeYay*...for being my best nerdy friend and for always supporting me.

Thank you, cousin *"Patty" Pritchett-Alexander*, for supplying me with the information needed to recount the life and times of *Geneva* proudly and positively, even if just for this one fleeting moment in her life as a fictional character in a children's story. She is now and forever immortalized within the pages of this children's book. Thank you for the images of *Geneva* that placed a face with the name branding her image onto the hearts and pupils of all who gaze upon her beauty…a wide-eyed young woman who, although she fought a very diligent fight…eventually surrender under the malicious pressures of *Lupus*.

Posthumously I'd like to thank *Marie Polite*. Although sight unseen…ever…you've blessed me with the strength, compassion, kindness, determination, and diligent spirit of your daughter *Carphetis*. And it is for that reason, I must thank you…mom. I love you. Thank you *Peaches*, for gently yet sternly thrusting me forward to complete this story, to dismiss all distractions, to release all tensions, and stress, and to move forward towards a triumphant end…the publishing of this book, *"Amir's First Haircut."* Although "LIFE" continued to get in the way…you kept your palm pressed firmly in the pit of my back preventing me from moving backwards. Gently, you placed your hands on my cheeks and made me look forward, and never look away from my true mission…the completion of this book. And even after our baby, and furever best friend ResQ passed away, still, you made me see the importance of finishing this story without holding on to the pain perforated within both of our hearts. I thank you, and I love you…*Peaches*. Thank you, *Carl, our son*, for being our tall arms and long legs when the moment demanded that we stretch. *We love you, son.*

Thank you, *Nikki*, for keeping me in mind as my big sister, constantly showing your love by aiding in book signings, and other areas involving literary works. Thank you for helping with the latest book signing for all the books published. You're the bestest big sister…EVER!! I love you dear sister, for caring for *Mommie* in her time of need, and decorating my previous Book Signing, with the assistance of our niece, *Samelia "Mealie" Davis*, my grandniece *Karyss*, and our other niece *Vanessa "Shawnie" Core*. I love you all for making my dreams come true and for allowing me to concentrate on the signing instead of other trivial matters. I will always love you all for that. Thank you, *Leah Cross*, for standing by when I needed moral support, and a break to develop a fresh pair of eyes. Speaking with you nearly daily, gave my mind time to rejuvenate, and continue my writing with a breath of fresh air in my lungs, and bright whites in my eyes. We love you daughter. Thank you, *La Guardia, our second son* for holding down the fort, and keeping our daughter, *Leah*, and our grandbabies; *Amalah*, and *Nayely* smiling and laughing…along with millions logged on to the world wide web.

Thank you, *Brother Walton aka DJ Blak*, for spinning the best music at our previous book signing. Soulful international jazz and ol' school tunes that kept all the children dancing, and the heads of adults swaying to the rhythms. Thank you, my beautiful, and compassionate sister *Kamesha*, Goddaughters *NaDayja* and *Jasha*, and Godson *Handsom* for lending all your support. You're some of the best Godchildren ever. Thank you, *Oscar Jr.,* for always being there in my time of need, safely transporting me to and from events and being my biologically linked Knight in Shining Armor. I love you, *cousin Junnii*. Thank you, *Darryl Lacy*, for always standing a little to the left, and watching out for your dear *Sister'Fam*. I love you…even though you made me read at my book signing unprepared, knowing I stutter and hate reading in public…**THANKS BRUHMAN!!!** But seriously, thank you for making me do that. I felt like a roller-skater falling on my butt for the first time…it wasn't as bad as I envisioned. I love you *Darryl*.

Thank you, my brother *Amir, MC Spice" Shakir*, your beautiful wife/my sister *Cashawna*, and your beautiful and talented genius of a daughter, *Ayah*, for believing in my literary prowess, and supporting me all the way, especially via Social Media {Instagram}. Thank you to our brothers: *Mark* and his loving husband *David*, for always coming to our events and supporting in ways only they know how. A warm thank you to our special ladies: *Maryann*, and our other sister, *Joann* for always making sure to attend every event we host, albeit literary or festive. We love you ladies like cooked food…and you've seen me, so you know how much I love cooked food. {smile}.

Speaking of "FOOD…"

A huge thank you to our culinary sister, *Alabama Dot* {you know who you are} for always catering our events both literary and festive with the best soul-food imaginable. We love you for always supporting the releases of each Dumplinz book as it is published. We will never forget your kind and loving support. Furthermore, a huge thank you goes out to our other loving culinary sister, *Tonya "Sinful Delights" Burrell*, for constantly supporting us with fantastic treats and for catering private romantic events like no other caterer.

An enormous sincere and loving debt of gratitude to everyone who has taken the time to purchase all my books throughout the years. I appreciate and love you all. To all the children about to read this book, and to all the parents who take the time to read this book to their children…I pray…

May All Your Hopez N' Dreamz Come True!

"Hope Syndreamz"

www.ingramcontent.com/pod-product-compliance
Lightning Source LLC
Chambersburg PA
CBHW061145010526
44118CB00026B/2874